# King David & the National Treasure

An **EASY KIDS MUSICAL**

about **WORSHIPING GOD**

Created by Pamela Vandewalker and Cherry Garasi

lillenaskids.com

# CONTENTS

Intro/Cast/Props . . . . . 3

**Praise Parade** . . . . . 4

Scene 1 . . . . . 6

**The Treasure of Our Nation** . . . . . 7

Scenes 2 & 3 . . . . . 9

**Go Back to the Word** . . . . . 10

Scene 4 . . . . . 12

**Great Shepherd** . . . . . 13

Scene 5 . . . . . 15

**Praise Parade (Reprise)** . . . . . 16

Scene 6 . . . . . 18

**Worship We Bring** . . . . . 18

Song Devotionals . . . . . 22

# *King David & The National Treasure*

Bible Story
*II Samuel 6:1-19*

King David loved and trusted God; he wanted to show His love for God by bringing the Ark of gold to Jerusalem so that the city would be a city of worship. He knew the Ark had been in Kiriath-Jearim (kihr'ee-ath-JEE-uh-rim) for twenty years. He talked to important leaders in Israel about bringing the Ark to Jerusalem and they liked the King's suggestion.

David planned to make the bringing of the Ark to the city a big celebration with dancing, instruments and singing. He had the Ark put on a cart that oxen would pull. Many people walked along side the cart singing and shouting with joy. In one place the road was rough and the oxen stumbled. Uzza, one of the men driving the oxen, put out his hand to steady the Ark. When his hand touched the Ark, Uzza died instantly. David and the Israelites were frightened; they didn't want to take the Ark one step further so they took it to the nearest house.

The Ark stayed there for three months. God greatly blessed the family where the Ark was housed. During that time David, found out more information about the Ark. David had forgotten that God gave careful instructions about how to move the Ark. Only the Levites were allowed to carry the Ark with poles. They were to carry the poles on their shoulders. God gave these rules to remind the Israelites that He is holy and His Ark is set apart.

After these three months passed, David wanted to bring the Ark into Jerusalem. So he gathered the Israelites together and the Levites carefully carried the Ark on their shoulders with poles, as God commanded, into Jerusalem. David and the Israelites danced and sang for joy. They brought the Ark to Jerusalem and David appointed some Levites to take care of the Ark and God's people worshiped Him.

## Cast

| | |
|---|---|
| PETER | Upbeat TV announcer *(Optional adult)* |
| ABIGAIL | Upbeat TV announcer *(Optional adult)* |
| HAL HERALD | King David's spokesperson |
| DAVID | King of Israel |
| NATHAN | David's trusted advisor |
| ABINADAB | Israelite |

## Props

Ark of the Covenant – gold chest
Wagon – to transport the Ark
Two gold poles – to transport the chest

## Optional Props

Banners
Rhythm instruments

# Praise Parade

*CD POINTS: Split-channel, CD:1-7; Stereo Trax, CD:8-14

25
E♭
A♭
Wor-ship with shouts!
A - men Praise God!
Cym-bals and horns!
28
B♭sus
C sus
C
Lift our ban - ners high!
32
F
Praise pa-rade,
praise pa-rade;
I'm march-ing in the
35
C
A 7
D m
praise pa-rade.
Come march a - long
from the east and the west;
38
G 7
C
N.C.
Sing to the Lord 'cause He's the best of the best.
41
F
Praise pa-rade,
praise pa-rade;
Hal - le - lu - jah for the
44
C
A 7
D m
praise pa-rade.
Come on and join from here and ev - 'ry-where;
47
G 7
C
Sing to the Lord 'cause none can com-pare.
51
F
C
F
Praise pa-rade,
praise pa-rade;
It's a praise pa - rade!

## SCENE 1 – Parade Route

*(After the song "Praise Parade," Choir processes to the stage during the song with the Ark being pulled in a wagon. Selected children with the Ark wait offstage during the following dialogue.)*

PETER: This is Peter Paul with PRAISE news and I'm here live from the parade route in Nacon. I've got to tell you, Abigail, this is the largest parade I've ever seen.

ABIGAIL: You're right! I've never seen so many people in one place before; there are dancers, singers and bands from Dan to Beersheba.

PETER: Absolutely, Abigail . . . all of this excitement is because King David is having the Ark of the Covenant brought into the capital city of Jerusalem. And it's headed this way . . . the crowd is going crazy . . . can't wait to get a glimpse of the Ark.

ABIGAIL: One word describes this scene: JOY!

PETER: Earlier King David's spokesperson, Hal Herald, began the day with this statement; let's listen:

HAL: Thank you for coming from all the territories of Israel today. As you know, we all agreed that it would be good to move the Ark of the Covenant back into Jerusalem. And now it's time. This ark is our national treasure and it needs to be in Jerusalem to make our great city the center of worship of the only true God.

*(Choir ad lib shouts.)*

PETER: So with those words the Ark of the Covenant was placed on a new constructed cart with Uzzah and Ahio guiding the special box.

ABIGAIL: Peter, what exactly is the Ark of the Covenant?

PETER: I'm glad you asked, Abigail!

# The Treasure of Our Nation

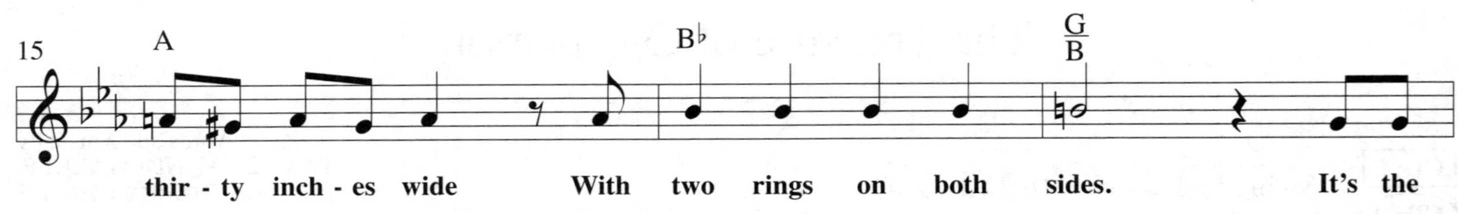
15
A
B♭
G
B
thir - ty inch - es wide With two rings on both sides. It's the

18
C m
F m
B♭
D
E♭
G sus
treas - ure of our na - tion re - mind - ing us that God is the One–

21
G
mf
1, 2
C m
G 7
(to pg. 7, meas. 5)
The on - ly true God.

24
3
C m
G 7
mp
C m
God. The on - ly true God.

27
G 7
C m
N.C.
C m
The on - ly true God.

## SCENE 2 – Parade Route

ABIGAIL: We do have a national treasure on our hands!

PETER: As the Ark begins to make its way around the bend of the threshing floor here in Nacon, we have an exclusive interview with Abinadab. The Ark has been at his home in Judah. Abinadab, how long has the ark been with your family?

ABINADAB: 20 years and I want to tell you . . . God has blessed my family in a big way!

ABIGAIL: Why do you think this prosperity has occurred?

ABINADAB: Because God's presence is all over the Ark; that's one powerful box!

ABIGAIL: Well, thank you! *(Putting hand up to ears as if listening to inner ear device; pause)* Oh my, something has just happened on the parade route. It seems . . . *(clearly shaken)* It seems there has been some sort of accident with the Ark of the Covenant . The parade has stopped!

PETER: We are receiving unconfirmed reports that casualties have been reported.

ABIGAIL: We will sort out the details and get back to you.

**CD: 3** **CD: 10** SFX: Praise News Theme Music

## SCENE 3 – In David's Palace

DAVID: Nathan, it has been a month and I'm still confused and upset; I can't believe that I caused that tragedy in the accident with the Ark. I thought I was doing the right thing. I just wanted everyone to worship God and I thought bringing the Ark to Jerusalem would be a good thing. I really don't understand why God would let this happen.

NATHAN: King David, God's ways are higher than ours and not always for us to understand. But, in this case, I think God made His intentions very clear.

DAVID: What are you saying?

NATHAN: Why don't you go back to the Word . . . you know, the laws that Moses gave us and see what it says about the Ark of the Covenant . . . see what instructions God gave our people about the Ark.

DAVID: There are instructions? Who reads instructions?

NATHAN: That's a question that will be debated for centuries. *(Pause)* My suggestion, David, is for you to go back to the Word . . . God's Word!

# Go Back to the Word

Words and Music by
PAMELA VANDEWALKER
and CHERRY GARASI

Do Not Photocopy

18 F GROUP 1 GROUP 2 GROUP 1
Go back to the Word! (Go back to the Word!) Hey, hey, hey, hey!
21 B♭7 GROUP 2 GROUP 1 F GROUP 2
(Hey, hey, hey, hey!) Go back to the Word! (Go back to the Word!)
24 F ALL C7
Hey, have - n't you heard? Go back to the Word!
26 B♭7 F
Go back to the Word!
28 N.C. C7
Hey, have - n't you heard? Go back to the Word!
30 B♭7 F N.C.
Go back to the Word! *Go back!*

## SCENE 4 – In David's Palace

DAVID: Nathan, Nathan – I don't know why I didn't go to God's Word to begin with; I blew it big time. But I have followed your advice in these past months; I've been studying the Word.

NATHAN: What did you learn, King David?

DAVID: I did it all wrong; I had the Ark carried on a wagon by good people but not consecrated people. God clearly says that the Ark must be carried on poles by Levites. It is holy and cannot be touched. I've learned a great lesson. *(Stand and pause)* Nathan . . . please tell the Levites to prepare for worship; now is the time to bring the Ark to Jerusalem . . . the right way.

NATHAN: As you wish, great King.

DAVID: I'm truly sorry for what I caused.

NATHAN: God knows and He forgives you, King. He sees your heart and knows you seek after Him. But it is always good to be reminded that God is holy. He wants us to spend time seeking His heart everyday so that praise and worship will flow from us as we follow Him.

DAVID: Yes, I now understand worship with good intentions isn't enough; God deserves worship with obedience. The Lord God has always shown me His way when I seek Him.

# Great Shepherd

Words and Music by
PAMELA VANDEWALKER
and CHERRY GARASI

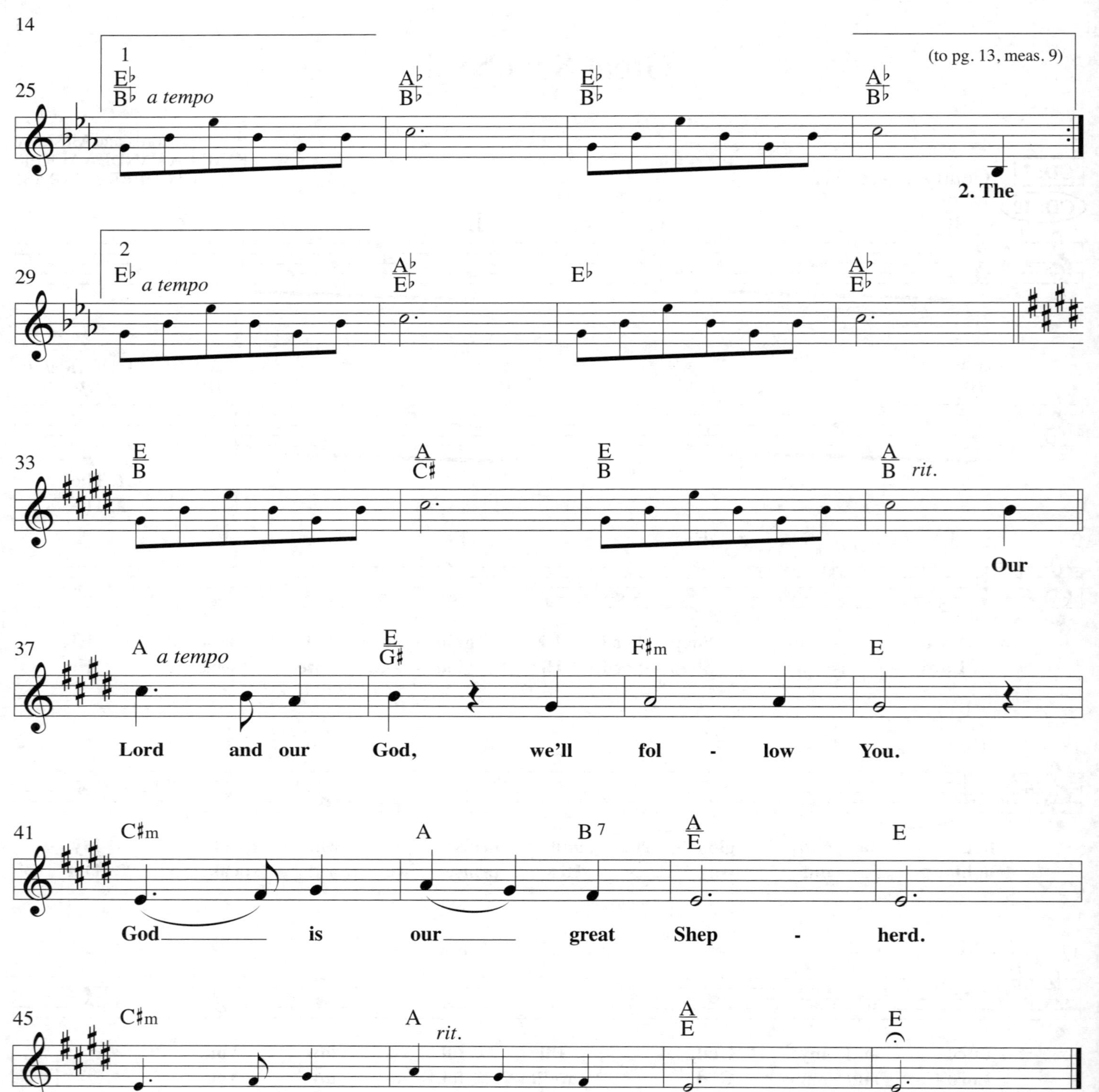
(to pg. 13, meas. 9)
a tempo
2. The
a tempo
rit.
Our
a tempo
Lord and our God, we'll fol - low You.
God is our great Shep - herd.
rit.

## SCENE 5 – Parade Route

PETER: It has been three months since we began to follow the story of the return of the Ark of the Covenant to Jerusalem. This extraordinary chest has been with the family of Obed-Edom, from Gath, for these three months and God has blessed this family in a big way.

ABIGAIL: That's right, today is the day that King David and his entourage are bringing the Ark into Jerusalem. King David's spokesperson, Hal Herald, has these words for us:

HAL: Today our great King has assembled all Israel to bring up the Ark of the Lord to a special place in Jerusalem. He has summoned the priests and the Levites to lead the parade with singing accompanied by instruments.

*(Choir ad lib shouts)*

PETER: Wow, Abigail. This parade may be bigger than the first. There are people everywhere!

ABIGAIL: Indeed there are, Peter! What a sight to see!

*(Selected children carry the Ark on pole to center stage during song.)*

# Praise Parade (Reprise)

Words and Music by
PAMELA VANDEWALKER,
CHERRY GARASI
and JUDY C. WAHLBOM

25
E♭
Wor-ship with shouts!
A - men Praise God!
A♭
Cym-bals and horns!
28
B♭sus
C sus
C
Lift our ban-ners high!
32
F
Praise pa-rade, praise pa-rade; I'm march-ing in the
35
C
A 7
D m
praise pa-rade. Come march a-long from the east and the west;
38
G 7
C
N.C.
Sing to the Lord 'cause He's the best of the best.
41
F
Praise pa-rade, praise pa-rade; Hal-le-lu-jah for the
44
C
A 7
D m
praise pa-rade. Come on and join from here and ev-'ry-where;
47
G 7
C
Sing to the Lord 'cause none can com-pare.
51
F
C
F
Praise pa-rade, praise pa-rade; It's a praise pa-rade!

## SCENE 6 - Parade Route

DAVID *(with arms raised high and boldly)*: Friends . . . we worship a great God, who alone is worthy to be praised! Join me and shout praise to the Lord our God!

ALL: Yea God! Praise God! Yea God!

DAVID: From this day forward, we will praise God's power, majesty, mercy and love. We give thanks and praise in song for great is the Lord!

# Worship We Bring

Words and Music by
PAMELA VANDEWALKER
and CHERRY GARASI

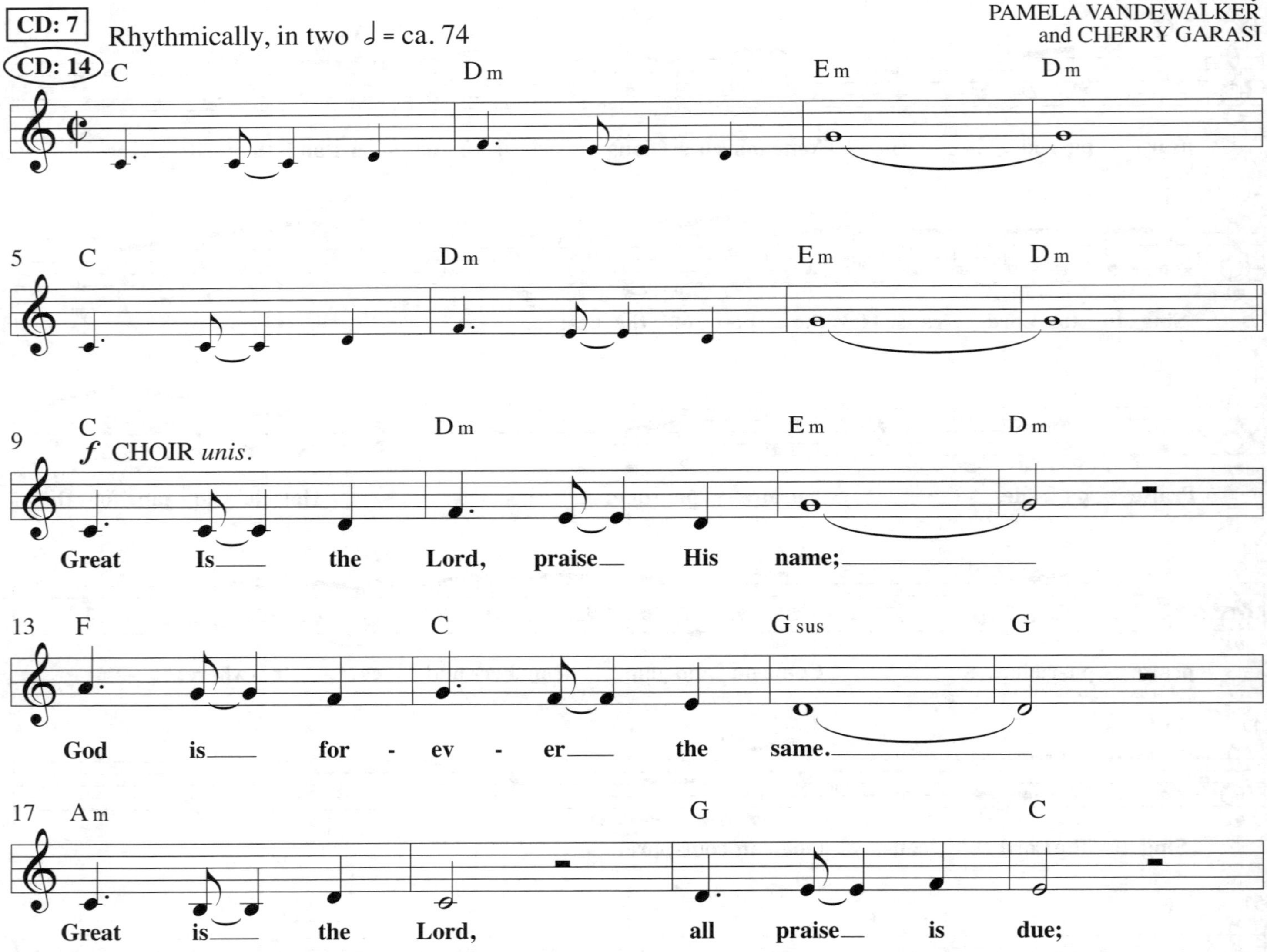

CD: 7

CD: 14

Rhythmically, in two 𝅗𝅥 = ca. 74

C Dm Em Dm

C Dm Em Dm

C Dm Em Dm

*f* CHOIR *unis.*

Great Is the Lord, praise His name;

F C Gsus G

God is for - ev - er the same.

Am G C

Great is the Lord, all praise is due;

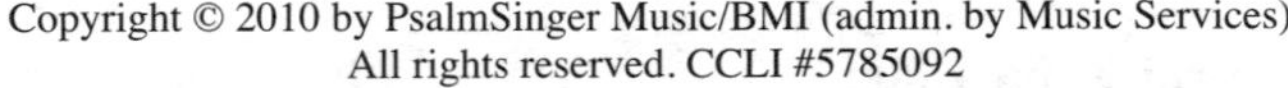

21 F C G sus G
His faith - ful love is so true.
25 Am Em F C
Praise glo - ry and hon - or; His great name we sing.
29 Am Em F G
Praise glo - ry and hon - or; wor - ship we bring.
33 Am Em F C
Praise glo - ry and hon - or; His great name we sing.
37 Am Em F G
Praise glo - ry and hon - or; wor - ship we bring.
41 Am Em F G C
Give praise to our God for all He's done.
45 Am Em F
(to meas. 25)
Make His glo - ry known 'cause He's the One we

49
DESCANT
f
Hon - or, glo - ry,
CHOIR
Am Em F C
Praise glo - ry and hon - or; His great name we sing.

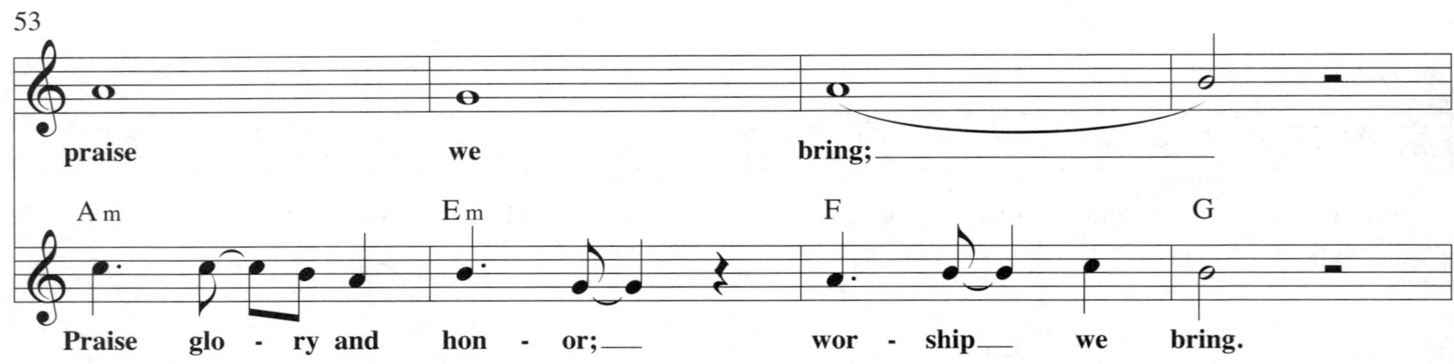
53
praise we bring;
Am Em F G
Praise glo - ry and hon - or; wor - ship we bring.

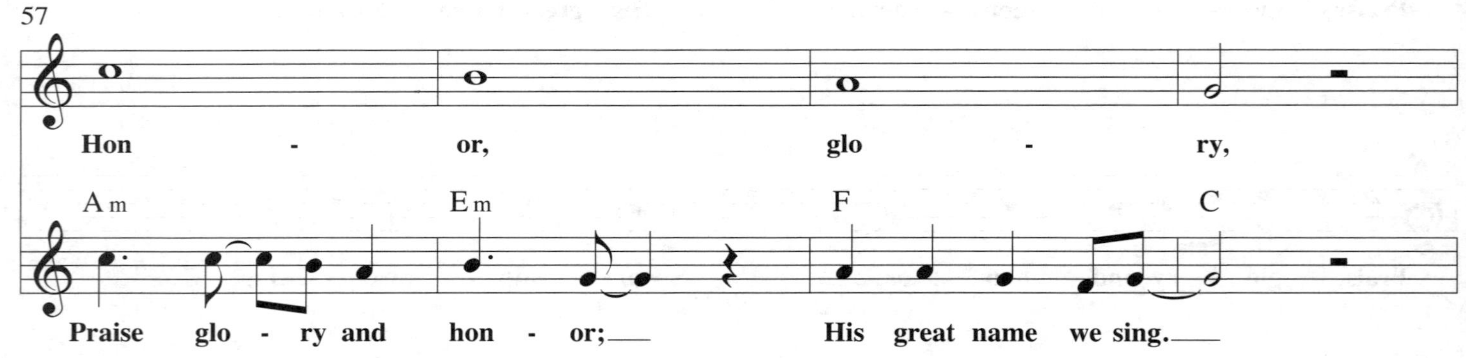
57
Hon - or, glo - ry,
Am Em F C
Praise glo - ry and hon - or; His great name we sing.

61
molto rit.
praise and wor - ship, we bring.
Am Em F G C
Praise glo - ry and hon - or; wor - ship we bring.

# "PRAISE PARADE"
# Devotional

**"What's the WORD?" . . . about Praise.**

Maybe one of the first prayers you learned was:

*God is great, God is good; Let us thank Him for our food.*
*By His hands we all are fed; Give us Lord, our daily bread. Amen.*

This prayer begins the way the Bible tells us we should begin every prayer to God – by praising Him! "Praise" is something that we give to those who deserve or earn that recognition. Because of all the things God is, and because of what He has done, God is the only One who always deserves your praise. God's Word says you were actually created for that very reason – to praise Him.

Why should you praise God? For these reasons:

God is love
God is good
God provides everything you need
God created everything
God is always with you
God cares about you
God heals you
God protects you
God is great and powerful
God knows everything
God has a special plan for you

Praise God every day – in what you say, think, and do.

# "Praise Parade" Scriptures

(All NIV)

- Sing to him, sing praise to him; tell of all his wonderful acts.
  *1 Chronicles 16:9*

- Among the gods there is none like you, O Lord; no deeds can compare with yours.
  *Psalm 86:8*

- Clap your hands, all you nations; shout to God with cries of joy.
  *Psalm 47:1*

- Shout with joy to God, all the earth!
  *Psalm 66:1*

- We will shout for joy when you are victorious and will lift up our banners in the name of our God. *Psalm 20:5*

- Praise the LORD. Praise God in his sanctuary; praise him in his mighty heavens.
  Praise him with the sounding of the trumpet, praise him with the harp and lyre,
  Praise him with tambourine and dancing, praise him with the strings and flute,
  Praise him with the clash of cymbals, praise him with resounding cymbals.
  Let everything that has breath praise the LORD. Praise the LORD.
  *Psalm 150:1, 3-6*

# "THE TREASURE OF OUR NATION"
## Devotional

**"What's the WORD?" . . . about the Ark of the Covenant.**

When I was a girl (child), I had a "Keepsake Box." In that box, I put all the things that were special or important to me: letters from my friends and family, seashells I found at the beach, jewelry, and a few things I had made in church or school. I decorated the box with gold paint, pink flowers and glitter. The box was very special to me – the things that I kept in the box were special, but the box itself was a treasure to me because of what it meant. It represented memories and feelings and words that had become a part of my life.

When God told His people to put the stone tablets, on which Moses wrote God's commandments, Aaron's staff, and the gold jar of manna into a box, He also told the people how to decorate the box. God knew that in order for the people to think of the box as "special," they needed to see its beauty and the specific details of God's design. Just like my little homemade box, the Ark of the Covenant was a symbol of something special. The things in the box were special in their own right. But, the Ark itself was sacred because it symbolized God's very presence with the people of Israel.

God was always with the people of Israel and He is always with you.

# "The Treasure of Our Nation" Scriptures

(All NIV)

- Have them make a chest of acacia wood-two and a half cubits long, a cubit and a half wide, and a cubit and a half high. Overlay it with pure gold, both inside and out, and make a gold molding around it. Cast four gold rings for it and fasten them to its four feet, with two rings on one side and two rings on the other. *Exodus 25:10-12*

- There, above the cover between the two cherubim that are over the ark of the Testimony, I will meet with you and give you all my commands for the Israelites. *Exodus 25:22*

- Behind the second curtain was a room called the Most Holy Place, which had the golden altar of incense and the gold-covered ark of the covenant. This ark contained the gold jar of manna, Aaron's staff that had budded, and the stone tablets of the covenant. *Hebrews 9:3-4*

# "GO BACK TO THE WORD"
## Devotional

**"What's the WORD?" . . . about the Bible – God's Word.**

Have you ever purchased something new at your house – a toy, or something Mom or Dad needed like shelves, or electronics – and it came with "instructions" for putting it together? In my family, my Dad never liked to read the directions for anything! Sometimes, after trying to make something work, or putting it together on his own, he would have to start all over and go back to read the instructions. We laughed with him for thinking he knew what to do without reading the directions. When you do not follow the directions for putting together a toy, or for working with electronics, it is sometimes funny. But, it is never funny when you do not follow God's instructions. King David discovered that when you do not follow God's Word, there are bad consequences.

Just as God gave clear instructions for how to move the Ark of the Covenant, He gives you rules and instructions for how to live your life. God always knows what is best for you. He knows that there are some things you should do, and some things you should not do. He gives rules and instructions so that you will follow Him and His plan for your life. When you do, everything works and fits together and you are able to live a life that is pleasing to God.

# "Go Back to the Word" Scriptures

(All NIV)

- Your word is a lamp to my feet and a light for my path.
  *Psalm 119:105*

- The LORD is my strength and my shield; my heart trusts in him, and I am helped. My heart leaps for joy and I will give thanks to him in song. *Psalm 28:7*

- I am making a way in the desert and streams in the wasteland.
  *Isaiah 43:19*

- For the word of God is living and active. Sharper than any double-edged sword, it penetrates even to dividing soul and spirit, joints and marrow; it judges the thoughts and attitudes of the heart. *Hebrews 4:12*

- All Scripture is God-breathed and is useful for teaching, rebuking, correcting and training in righteousness. *2 Timothy 3:16*

# "GREAT SHEPHERD"
## Devotional

**"What's the WORD?" . . . about the Great Shepherd.**

When King David was a boy, he was a shepherd. Sheep do not have very good instincts of their own, so they must have someone to provide the basic things they need to live. A shepherd's job is to take care of a herd of sheep – when they are outside grazing and drinking in the daytime, or sleeping in the night. A shepherd can never sleep because he must always be alert for any danger that may come to his sheep. David cared for his father's sheep from the time he was a small boy and he understood what it meant to provide safety, guidance, food, water and shelter for his flock.

David was also a musician. The Bible tells us that he played his harp as he sat on the hillsides all alone with his sheep and he sang praise songs to God. Even as a small boy, David knew that God loved him and had a special plan for his life. David wrote a beautiful Psalm about God being his Shepherd. Find Psalm 23 in your Bible and read the words out loud. As you read, think about the goodness of God and how He cares for you.

# "Great Shepherd" Scriptures

(All NIV)

- The LORD is my shepherd, I shall not be in want. He makes me lie down in green pastures, he leads me beside quiet waters, he restores my soul. He guides me in paths of righteousness for his name's sake.

  Even though I walk through the valley of the shadow of death, I will fear no evil, for you are with me; your rod and your staff, they comfort me. You prepare a table before me in the presence of my enemies. You anoint my head with oil; my cup overflows.

  Surely goodness and love will follow me all the days of my life, and I will dwell in the house of the LORD forever. *Psalm 23*

- My mouth will speak in praise of the LORD. Let every creature praise his holy name forever and ever. *Psalm 145:21*

- The LORD will guide you always. *Isaiah 58:11*

# "WORSHIP WE BRING"
## Devotional

**"What's the WORD?" . . . about Worship.**

What does it mean to worship God? You can begin to understand what it means when you understand who God is. The Bible says God made us "in His own image." God made you. He is a great, powerful and loving God. Because He is all these things, you worship Him.

You can sing joyful songs of praise to God. You can worship Him by playing instruments and with dancing just like King David and the people of Israel. Worship is completely focusing on God. You can worship God in many ways. You can also worship God by thinking about Him all through the day. Sometimes you may look at the beauty of nature outside and it may make you think of the goodness of God.

Another way to worship God is to pray. When you pray, you are talking straight to God and He speaks to you. When you pray, you should always let Him know how much you love Him and how thankful you are for all He has done. God deserves our worship. He deserves all of you – your thoughts, your actions and your love.

# "Worship We Bring" Scriptures

(All NIV)

- Give thanks to the LORD, call on his name; make known among the nations what he has done. Sing to him, sing praise to him; tell of all his wonderful acts. Glory in his holy name; let the hearts of those who seek the LORD rejoice. *1 Chronicles 16:8-10*

- Sing to the LORD, all the earth; proclaim his salvation day after day. Declare his glory among the nations, his marvelous deeds among all peoples. For great is the LORD and most worthy of praise; he is to be feared above all gods. *1 Chronicles 16:23-25*

- Ascribe to the LORD the glory due his name. Bring an offering and come before him; worship the LORD in the splendor of his holiness. *1 Chronicles 16:29*

- Give thanks to the LORD, for he is good; his love endures forever. *1 Chronicles 16:34*

- Praise be to the LORD, the God of Israel, from everlasting to everlasting. *1 Chronicles 16:36*